yukismart.com/b/6e00d6
AF364351
1
2

**pineapple**
สับปะรด
*sapparot*

**guitar**
กีตาร์
*kita*

# 2

two
สอง
*song*

**dinosaurs**
ไดโนเสาร์

*dainosao*

**twins**
ฝาแฝด

*fafaet*

# three

## สาม

*sam*

# starfishes

## ปลาดาว

*pladao*

# peaches

## พีช

*phicha*

# four
# สี
*si*

# cherries
# เชอร์รี
*choeri*

# robots
# หุ่นยนต์
*hunyon*

# 5

five

ห้า

*ha*

## fingers

นิ้ว

*nio*

## pencils

ดินสอ

*dinso*

# 6

six

หก

*hok*

## candies

ลูกอม

*luk-om*

## hearts

หัวใจ

*huachai*

# 7

seven

เจ็ด

*chet*

## seashells

เปลือกหอย

*plueakhoi*

## blocks

บล็อก

*blok*

# 8

**eight**

แปด

*paet*

## ants

มด

*mot*

## flowers

ดอกไม้

*dokmai*

# 9

**nine**

เก้า

*kao*

**fishes**

ปลา

*pla*

**buttons**

กระดุม

*kradum*

# 10

**candles**
เทียน

*thian*

**eggs**
ไข่

*khai*

2 4 6 8 10

**even**

เลขคู่

*lekkhu*

1 3 5 7 9

**odd**

เลขคี่

*lekkhi*

# whole

ทั้งหมด

*thangmot*

# half

ครึ่ง

*khrueng*

red
แดง
daeng

umbrella
ร่ม
rom


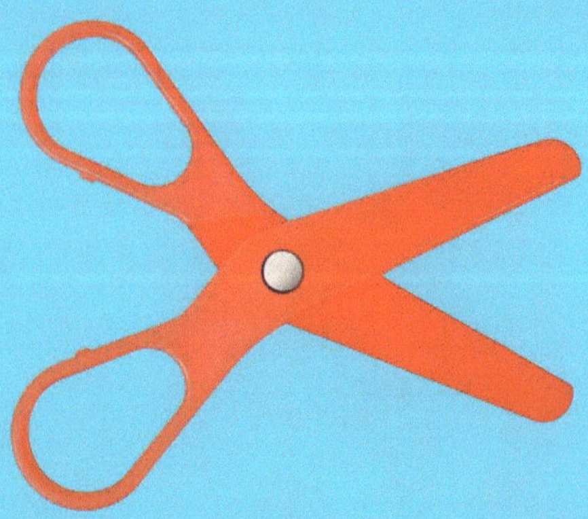


scissors
กรรไกร
kankrai

## yellow
เหลือง
*lueang*

## banana
กล้วย
*kluai*

## cheese
ชีส
*chit*

# green
## เขียว
*khiao*

# vegetables
## ผัก
*phak*

# bottle
## ขวด
*khuat*

# gray

เทา

*thao*

# carpet

พรม

*phrom*

# feather

ขนนก

*khon nok*

**orange**

ส้ม

*som*

**pumpkin**

ฟักทอง

*fakthong*

**orange juice**

น้ำส้ม

*namsom*

white

ขาว

*khao*

**cup**

ถ้วย

*thuai*

**envelope**

ซองจดหมาย

*songchotmai*

**black**

ดำ

*dam*

**glasses**

แว่นตา

*waenta*

**shirt**

เสื้อเชิ้ต

*sueachoet*

# brown
## น้ำตาล
*namtan*

# violin
## ไวโอลิน
*wai-olin*

# cake
## เค้ก
*khek*

# blue

ฟ้า

*fa*

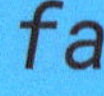

## swim shorts

กางเกงว่ายน้ำ

*kangkeng wainam*

## swimming goggles

แว่นตาว่ายน้ำ

*waenta wainam*

**pink**

ชมพู

*chomphu*

**ice cream**

ไอศกรีม

*aisakrim*

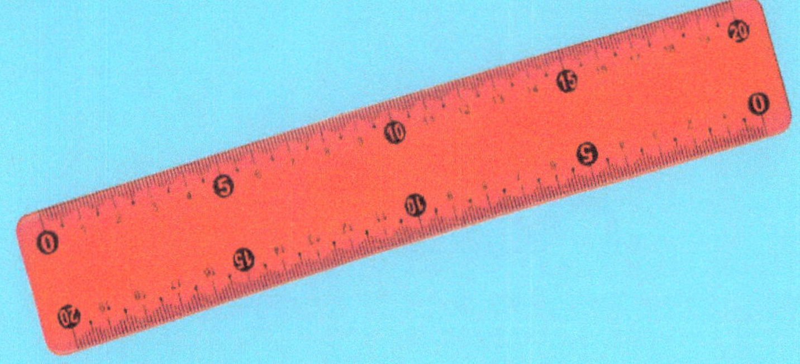

**ruler**

ไม้บรรทัด

*maibanthat*

**purple**

ม่วง

*muang*

**dice**

ลูกเต๋า

*luktao*

**fan**

พัด

*phat*

# light colors

## สีอ่อน

*si-on*

# dark colors

## สีเข้ม

*si khem*

## circle

วงกลม

*wongklom*

## square

สี่เหลียมจัตุรัส

*siliamchatturat*

## star

ดาว

*dao*

## heart

หัวใจ

*huachai*

## crescent
เสี้ยว

*siao*

## triangle
สามเหลียม

*samliam*

## rectangle
สีเหลียมผืนผ้า

*siliamphuenpha*

## oval
วงรี

*wongri*

**drop**
หยดน้ำ
*yotnam*

**cross**
กากบาท
*kakabat*

**cube**
ลูกบาศก์
*lukbat*

**sphere**
ทรงกลม
*songklom*

**ring**
วงแหวน
*wongwaen*

**trefoil**
ใบไม้สามแฉก
*baimai sam chaek*

**cylinder**
ทรงกระบอก
*songkrabok*

**cone**
กรวย
*kruai*

## line
เส้น

*sen*

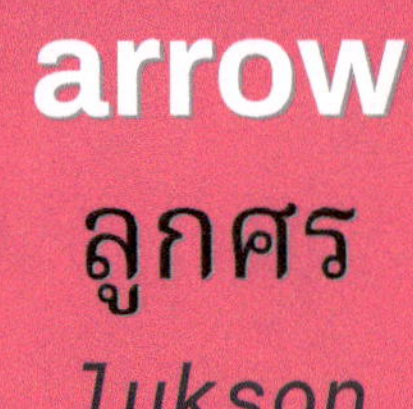

## arrow
ลูกศร

*lukson*

## dots
จุด

*chut*

**zigzag**

ซิกแซก

*siksaek*

**curve**

เส้นโค้ง

*senkhong*

**spiral**

เกลียว

*kliao*

# draw

## วาด

*wat*

# paint

## ระบาย

*rabai*

## count

นับ

*nap*

## write

เขียน

*khian*

**small**

เล็ก

*lek*

**big**

ใหญ่

*yai*

**mouse**

หนู

*nu*

**elephant**

ช้าง

*chang*

short

สั้น

*san*

long

ยาว

*yao*

worm

หนอน

*non*

snake

งู

*ngu*

**thin**

บาง

*bang*

**thick**

หนา

*na*

**empty**

ว่างเปล่า

*wangplao*

**full**

เต็ม

*tem*

1
2
3